What Grown-Ups Need to Know
About Art Therapy for Kids

By Kim L. Anderson

Published by

MabelMedia
InnerPrize Publishing*

Saint Louis, Missouri
ISBN 978-0-9718508-2-8

## Also by Kim Anderson

Culturally Considerate School
Counseling: Helping Without Bias

Creating Culturally Considerate Schools:
Educating Without Bias
(with Bonnie M. Davis)

Full Circle: Countertransference
Containment through Mandala-Making,
A Case Study of Closure

# Forward and Thanks

I truly enjoy working with kids. I did so early in my career as a family and child therapist and clinical social worker and again later, when I was finishing my training as an expressive arts psychotherapist. I continued working with kids until long after I was board certified as a registered art therapist.

One of the most challenging things for me about working with kids was their dependency – and therefore my clinical dependency – upon the grown-ups in their lives. Whether it was parents, grandparents, teachers, or foster care or case workers, grown-ups need to be involved in therapy for kids. It is difficult enough for grown-ups to understand the subtle benefits of child therapy, but it is sometimes even more difficult for them to understand art-making as a treatment modality and the art itself as a symbolic extension of the child or adolescent.

This book started out as a flyer I developed and included in the intake package when I would begin work with a new child client. It seemed useful and I began to share it with colleagues who also seemed to find it useful. I was encouraged to expand the content and include some examples that might illustrate the suggestions I made.

***What Grown-Ups Need to Know About Art Therapy for Kids*** is not intended to be a comprehensive textbook based in scholarly research but a readable and informed guidebook for any adult who is interested in supporting a child who is engaged in art therapy or perhaps even art-making in general. Many of the suggestions outlined may be used to encourage children's natural creativity and avoid unintentional interruption of talents, skills, and curiosities.

Although I had always invited creativity and the use of art-making in my practice, I decided to become trained as an art therapist because I wanted to be able to more completely appreciate and acknowledge the deep work embedded in the process of creating art. I also wanted to be able to be more informed in my responses in order to better guide my clients toward health and healing. Similarly, this book sets out to inform grown-ups about the process and promise of art therapy for kids and guide them in the support of their child's wellness.

I would like to acknowledge and thank those who gave support and imagination to this project. Kari Schepker-Mueller was a phenomenal resource and an enthusiastic supplier of exquisite images by her students at Maplewood Richmond Heights Middle School. She also enlisted the help of her colleagues and my thanks to Sally Saldana also shared the colors and textures of her students at MRH Elementary School. Likewise, Tom Butler introduced me to the art of his students at Glendale Elementary School, Glendale, Missouri. Special thanks to Kathy Graves, Brenda Alvarez, Eva Salome' A. Davis, Rick Sealey, Alysia Maggard, and my usual cheering section: Bonnie Davis, Deb Kuhn, Karen Friend Maggard and Bernard George Kuhn.

I am especially grateful to all of the young artists who agreed to illustrate these pages with their bright visions and the grown-ups in who understood the importance.

*Kim Anderson, December 2013*

# Part I – What is Art Therapy

The creative process is a natural one and has been an eternal outlet for personal feelings, internal conflicts, and issues involving family, community and social justice.

The American Art Therapy Association, defines art therapy as "a mental health profession in which clients, facilitated by the art therapist, use art media, the creative process, and the resulting artwork to explore their feelings, reconcile emotional conflicts, foster self-awareness, manage behavior and addictions, develop social skills, improve reality orientation, reduce anxiety, and increase self-esteem. A goal in art therapy is to improve or restore a client's functioning and his or her sense of personal well-being."

Children are naturally drawn to art as a way to engage with the world and learn from that engagement. They innately respond to the healing quality of creativity as a way to soothe and problem solve. Age, cognitive and emotional intelligence, maturity, stress, life experience and the "presenting issue" or stated reason for therapy determine the media by which clients express themselves and the manner in which they explore the process and the outcome. Young children may gravitate to crayons or finger paints. Adolescents may be attracted to oil pastels or computer graphics, choosing to depict music icons rather than superheroes as symbols to which they aspire.

# Part II – Who Offers Art Therapy?

While many child therapists and counselors use art and play as a means of connecting with child and adolescent clients, art therapy is a specific modality of treatment with specified standards. A master's degree in art therapy or a related field of study such as counseling, social work, or psychology is required for the practice of art therapy. If a therapist holds a master's degree in another field, s/he must also have additional post-graduate training and supervised experience in art therapy practice in order to be credentialed. These standards also include education and experience in art-making as well as in the therapeutic arts. Continuing education is required in order to maintain professional credentials in art therapy.

Some art therapists work in an office setting with a limited set of materials; others work in studio settings with a seemingly endless media supply. Therapists may differ in approach or method, but the basis of all art therapy is the use of art materials to convey emotion, consider options, and create change. The therapist's primary job is to validate the imagination by validating the images a child client brings to life.

# Part III – How Art Therapy Works

Judith Rubin wrote that "clinical work with children has always intertwined art and play." Art therapy and play therapy share a common bond through their natural appeal to children and the healing qualities of creativity, expression, fantasy, and safe communication. Both are spontaneous and self-generated, both self-expressive, and each practiced by children according to age, development, intellectual capacity, maturity, stress and life experience. Integrating art and play is intrinsic to any successful clinical work with children and requires that a warm and authentic relationship be developed between the child and therapist.

Art therapy involves verbal interaction between the therapist and child client and art-making by the child which serves to enhance the therapeutic conversation. Over time, the conversation may enhance the art. An art therapy office may be very different than other therapy offices. Art therapy materials are readily available, developmentally appropriate, varied, and intact. Space includes not only environment and lighting, but surfaces upon which to work, storage, and clean-up facilities. Order in organization of space and materials help to establish boundaries, frame, and safety. Safety means that all kind of expression is accepted, negative as well as positive, but also that limits are provided in order to protect a child from accidental or deliberate self-harm. Respect needs to be shown for the child's uniqueness through the freedom and choice allowed during process as well as respect for the art therapy product.

Interest in the child client must be communicated through sincerity, attentiveness, and appropriate verbal and affective responses. Pleasure should be expressed through enthusiastic appreciation of the child's effort and ability to approach both task and emotion. Support for the child's creativity, genuine empathy for his struggle to grow in and through art, and enhancement of expressive development are essential to the healing process of child art therapy.

The art therapist makes him/herself the ally of the child's creative venture, lending both technical assistance and emotional support, recognizing and responding to the hidden as well as overt aspects of the child's product and behavior. In art therapy, the creative process itself is central to the therapeutic encounter and the clinician's ability to facilitate that process is as important as her understanding of a child's visual communication.

In order to work with children successfully, the therapist must sincerely enjoy young people and take honest delight in their creative process. Because a child does not have the verbal capacity that adults possess, s/he

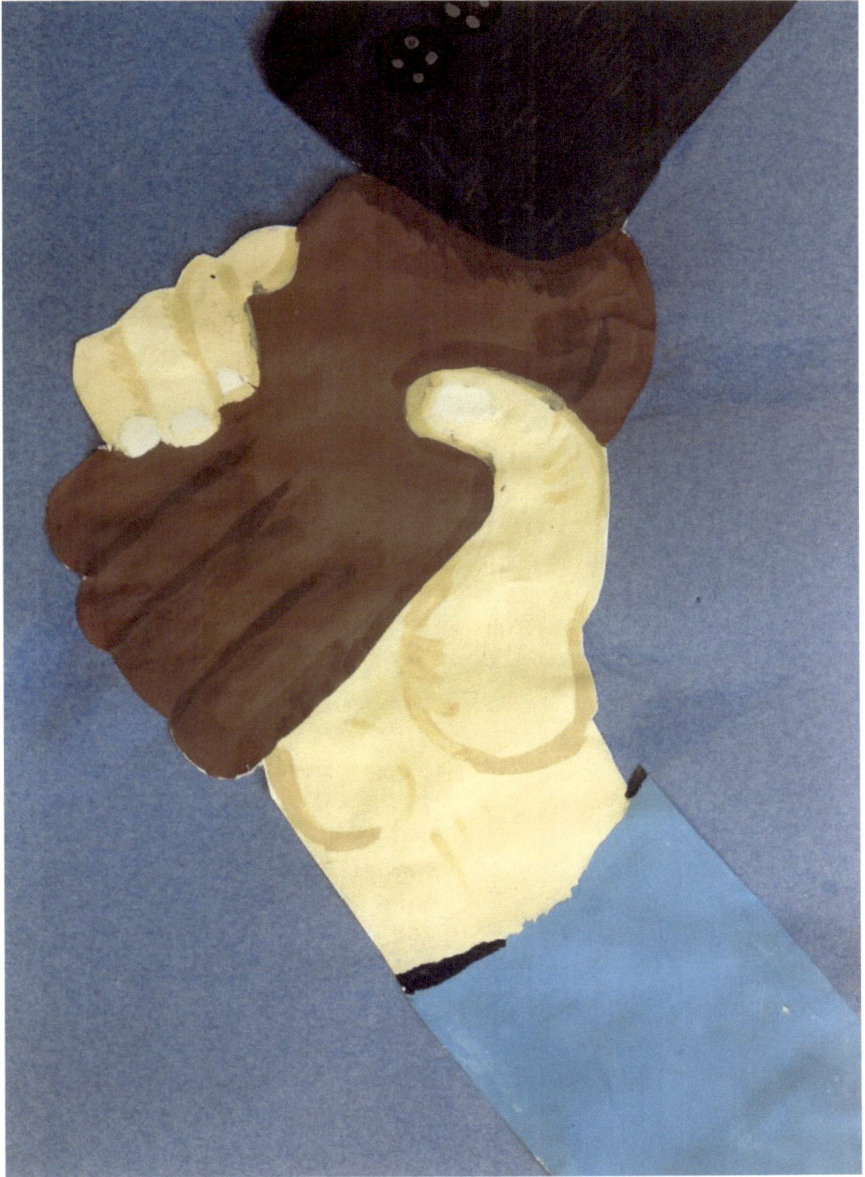

needs a therapist who can communicate and respond in non-verbal modalities. Movement, gesture, imagery, and sound are important elements as well as play. A therapist also must like the child within herself as (this) is a powerful tool in child art therapy.

There are also cautions to consider in the field of child art therapy. The use of touch for example has a very different meaning in work with children than in therapy with adults. A therapist must be able to convey nurturing warmth and comfort in a safe and supportive manner without threatening a child who may view physical contact as dangerous or provocative.

Some tenets of child therapy were outlined by Virginia Axline who wrote *Dibs in Search of Self*, a very memorable book about a young boy with autism and the story of his treatment, however some of these basic therapeutic principles may not always make sense to grown-ups who live with the child each day or must deal with the issues which have brought the child into therapy in the first place.

***The therapist must develop a warm, friendly relationship with the child in which a good rapport is established as soon as possible.***

Whether adult, child or adolescent, research shows the relationship between client and therapist to be the most important aspect of any therapy. This is especially true for children and teenagers. A child needs to feel that the person to whom s/he confides is genuine, inviting, and accessible. They also need to feel that the therapist has a sense of humor, even if they are there to talk about serious things. Sometimes grown-ups don't quite understand this. Sometimes they see it as being too nice to a child, especially if he or she has been brought to therapy because of conduct. Sometimes they are unfamiliar with how therapy works and think of it more as a consequence of bad behavior than an exploration of why a child has acted

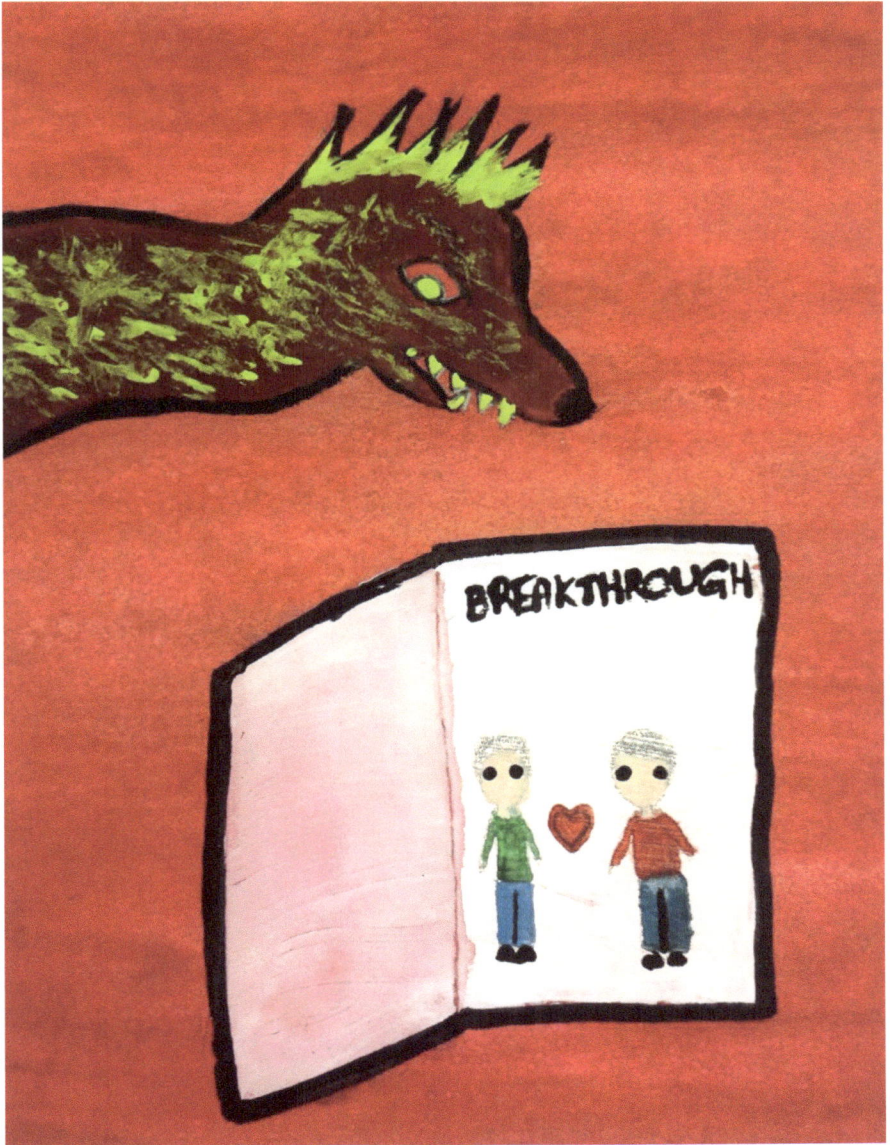

in a certain way. If a child is in treatment because something bad has happened, adults worry that the issues aren't being taken seriously if kids are having fun while being there. In rare instances, some parents even get a little jealous if a child can talk to another grown-up easier than they can talk to them.

It is important for grown-ups to know that therapy is about teaching children how to communicate more clearly with everyone in their lives – not just their art therapist. An important therapy goal is to not only learn what might be motivating a child, but help them to learn healthier ways of relating to people.

### The therapist accepts the child exactly as s/he is.

It is not unusual for a child or adolescent to come to art therapy because of a problem at school, behavior at home, or because of their "attitude." Approaching a child as if you expect trouble often only gets you trouble. Approaching a child with acceptance for who she is and how she relates to the world begins the long journey toward accepting herself.

Other grown-ups may not accept the behavior or the attitude a child displays, but one of the best things about therapy is that the child client and the therapist don't have to live together. It is much easier to accept behaviors or attitudes one hour a week than it is 24 hours a day. Because of this, it is also easier for the child to focus on feelings, understand them better, and make changes in how they deal with them.

### The therapist establishes a feeling of freedom in the relationship so that the child feels safe to express his or her feelings completely.

This means that children are free to be happy, sad, fearful or angry during his or her therapy, even if that means being angry at the therapist. Grown-ups may misunderstand some feelings such as fear or anger to mean that the therapy isn't working when, in fact, it is working well. It is important that the therapist sees any problematic behavior first hand – either in action or through art images.

### The therapist remains alert to the thoughts and feelings the child is expressing and reflects them back so that s/he may gain insight into problematic behavior.

The therapist needs to see any problematic behavior in the office in order to help the child redirect feelings, reorganize thinking, and learn to respond appropriately to challenging situations or people. If a parent or other adult becomes aware of this, they may reprimand the child or admonish them to be respectful of the therapist. This is neither necessary nor helpful in most instances because it interferes not only with the therapy process but in the relationship between therapist and child client. In the therapy space and time, the therapist must maintain the locus of control because while the child must have free reign to express him or herself. He must also feel that the therapist can catch him if he veers too far off the healing path.

*The therapist maintains a deep respect for the child's ability to solve problems if given an opportunity to do so.*

If you ask a child or adolescent to tell you why they think they are in therapy, they are generally honest and forthcoming. If you ask what they think needs to be done to solve the problem, they will also likely have some really good ideas. What they often lack is the ability to implement those ideas.

Art therapy is a ready-made modality for children and teens to learn problem solving. Children like to make things and they like to make them well. Even more important is making things work. Creating an art piece that does what the child wants it to do is one of the most meaningful outcomes of art therapy. Whether creating a five minute drawing that is so straightforward no one can mistake its meaning or a rainstick over three or four sessions and hearing the soothing rustle of the pebbles for the first time, kids like to succeed.

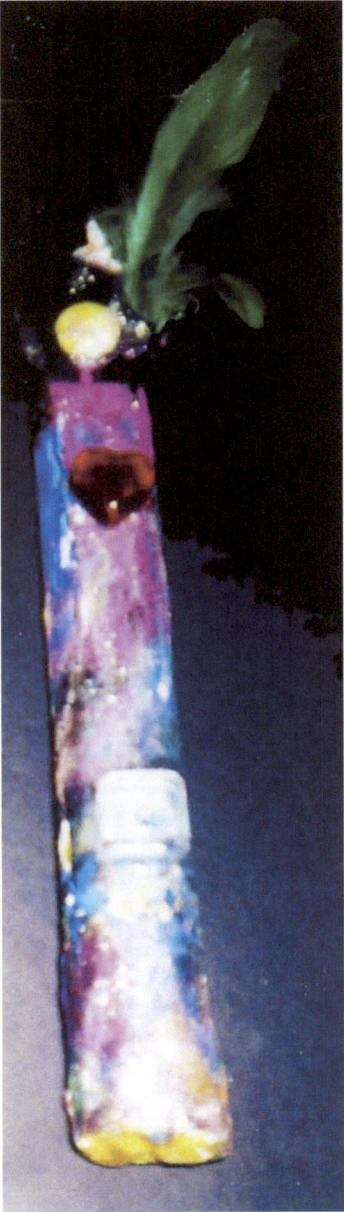

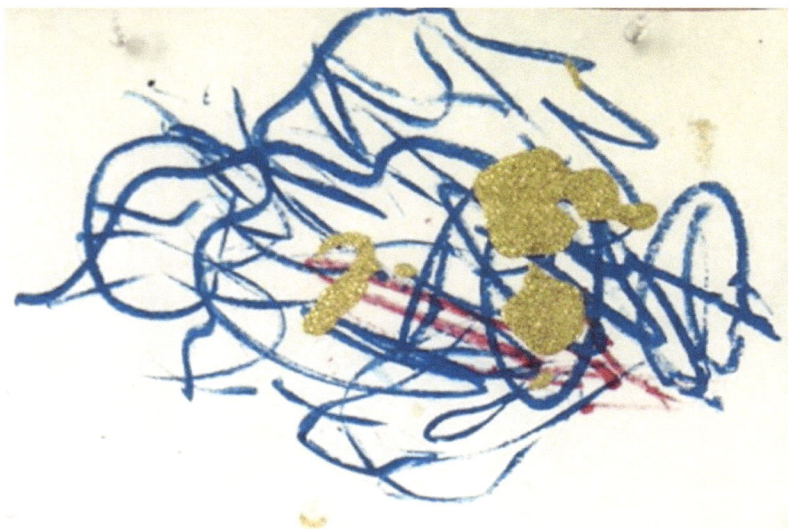

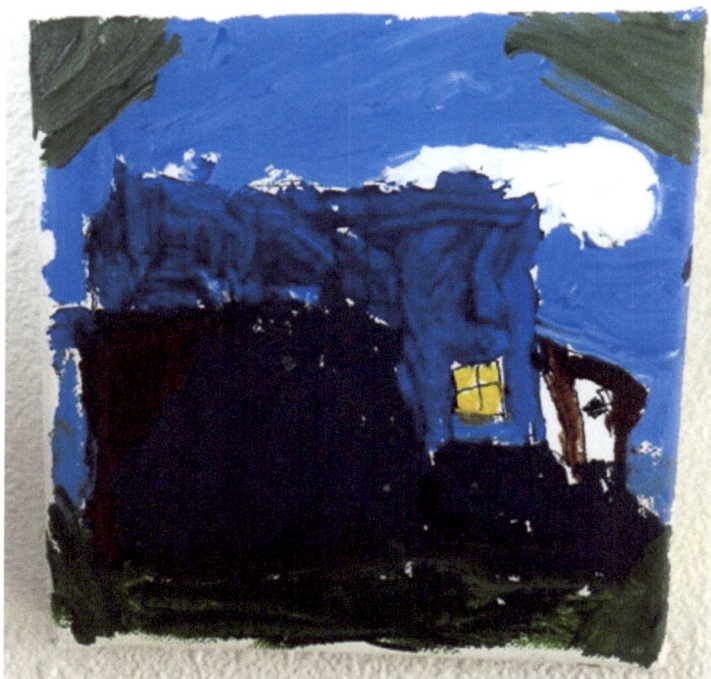

## The child leads the way; the therapist follows.

Although kids are most often physically transported to therapy by an adult who is concerned about them, they voluntarily decide whether to engage in the process or not. When they do, like adults, they are in charge of their treatment and a therapist must be willing to relinquish control in order for the child client to gain control.

Because so many children are brought to therapy by an adult who feels as if they have no control at all, this can be difficult for care-givers to understand.

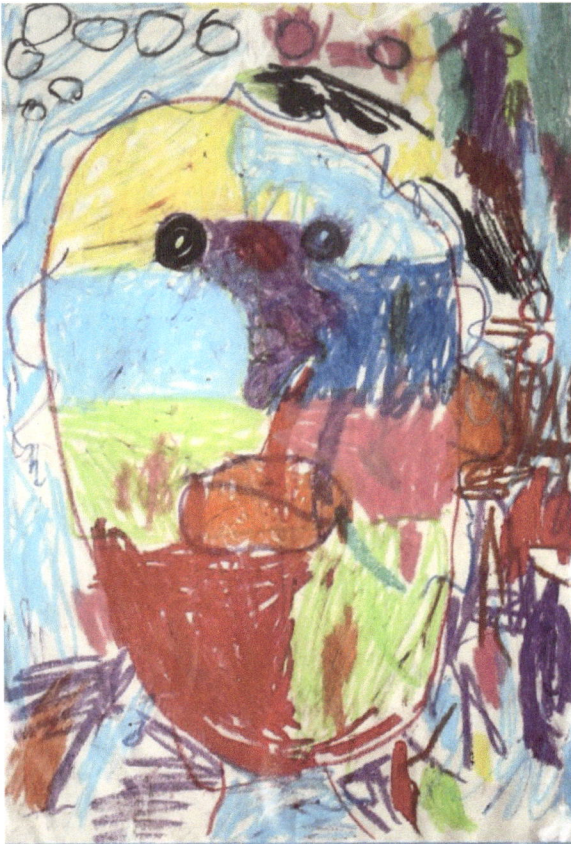

*The therapist does not attempt to hurry the therapy. It is a gradual process and is recognized as such.*

Kids have their own internal time clock. There are many factors that determine the pace of therapy. Age of the child, physical, cognitive and social development, learning style, environmental stability or disruption, and a child's own sense of urgency are a few of these factors. Rushing will do no good nor will lingering too long on unnecessary issues. In some instances, helping a child to understand there is no hurry is therapeutic in itself. This gives the message they can go at their own pace and master each step so they retain understanding and skills rather than hurrying on to the next level without a solid foundation.

*The therapist establishes only limitations that are necessary to anchor the therapy to the world of reality and to make the child aware of his/her responsibility in the relationship.*

As the therapy progresses, the art therapist must find ways to help kids take what they have learned into other relationships and other aspects of their lives. Through art, a child can develop autonomy and independence, taking responsibility for both process and (eventually) product. The meaning of the art activity changes as children mature. A "framework for freedom" illustrates conditions for growth and achievement of creative potential. This therapeutic framework is comprised of materials, space, time, order, safety, respect, interest, pleasure, and support.

# Part 4 – How Parents, Teachers and Other Adults Can Support a Kid in Art Therapy

The most important thing a grown-up needs to know about art therapy for kids is that it offers one of the best ways for a child to feel at home within a therapeutic context. Because art-making is a naturally occurring way for a child or adolescent to communicate his or her feelings and thoughts, art therapy invites the child client into a comfortable environment filled with familiar tools for health and healing. But just because it's an easy fit doesn't mean it isn't hard work.

*Children need consistency. Once therapy has begun, if possible, establish a regular appointment day and time.*

As with all things, children and adolescents do best when their lives are predictable. Consistency, routines, and stability are extremely important, especially when there are problems or disruptions in the family or a child has experienced a loss. Being able to count on the adults in his or her life is comforting and reassuring.

Therapy is designed to be consistent and a reliable resource for clients of any age. These days, families almost always have a calendar that guides them. Kids and teens are used to regular schedules for school, sports, and after school activities. Making art therapy a regular part of the week not only makes it reliable, but makes it "normal."

28

**_Demonstrate the importance of the child by making his or her therapy a priority. Keep scheduled appointments. Arrive on time. Participate as requested._**

Grown-ups set examples for children and teenagers by modeling positive attitudes and behaviors. Showing respect for a therapist's time by making art therapy a priority relays the message that the therapist and child are doing something important. Keeping appointments and arriving on time signals that art therapy isn't to be rushed or haphazard. Participating in the processes shows a child that the adult in her life believes art therapy is worthwhile and the child's work there is important. By doing so, the child client may more easily believe herself to be important.

**_Reinforce that therapy is a positive experience of growth, not a punishment for bad behavior, even if behavior is the presenting issue._**

Many children enter art therapy because something negative has happened. In some cases this is a loss such as a death, a divorce, or relocation. In others, it may be behavior that has resulted in a negative consequence. In the latter circumstance, it is easy for a child or adolescent to associate therapy with a punishment rather than a resource. Communicating the distinction is fundamental. Sometimes adults have a difficult time knowing the difference if art therapy has been suggested by an outside source such as a school administrator or law enforcement.

*If you are a parent or primary guardian, participate in your child's sessions, especially if s/he asks. If the child shares his/her art, respond positively to the effort, not the outcome. Be appreciative that you are included.*

It is customary for the primary adults in a child's life to be included in his or her therapy at some point. This is typically because a child's progress needs to be monitored at home or at school, but also because issues may arise that are important for parents/guardians to know. In addition, reinforcing what a child or adolescent learns in therapy by implementing new systems at home is critical to lasting change and wellness.

One of the differences between art therapy and other child therapies is, of course, the use of art materials to facilitate the therapy process. In art therapy, it is not uncommon for the adults to be invited to make art as well. Family art therapy can be a powerful modality for families to see issues and problems and to make changes by first making them in art mediums. Sometimes grown-ups have more anxiety about this than kids, though. If this happens, it is important for the adult to try to push through his or her resistance and join in.


**Respect the child's decision to leave art at the therapy office or bring it home. If a child decides to bring art home, establish a safe and private place to store it.**

Art is always an extension of the artist. In art therapy, art is even more intertwined with and reflective of a child's emotional state, self-concept, and identity. The art a child creates in art therapy needs to be treated with the same care and dignity as the child herself.

Often the art therapist will have a place reserved for the art each child client has made, but sometimes kids will prefer to take their art home. The decision must be the child's.


**Don't insist on seeing a child's art. It's okay to ask and is good to show interest, but pushing a child to reveal an image before he or she is ready is not helpful.**

Verbal content in therapy is always confidential unless it involves the imminent threat of harm to self or others. Likewise, the art content that results from art therapy is confidential. Children and teenagers are encouraged to share their feelings and issues with trusted adults in their lives outside of therapy, but unless they are in danger of being hurt by someone or hurting themselves or anyone else, they must trust that what they talk about and what they create in therapy are kept private.

33

***Don't interpret a child's art. Always allow him or her to tell you about the art they have made.***

Art may be a literal depiction, but it is often symbolic. What may appear very clear to one person may mean something entirely different to another. This is especially true when it comes to the art kids make and what adults see in it. Regardless of what we may think, have heard or been taught, themes, colors or images are not always universal. Red does not reflect anger to everyone. Blue is not always sad or depressed.

There are some simple phrases that can be used to encourage a child to talk about his art. "I am really interested in what you made today. Would you please tell me about it?" or "I'm so glad you are sharing what you did in therapy yesterday. I'd like to know more about it." Another helpful practice is to have a specific time and way in which art therapy is discussed.

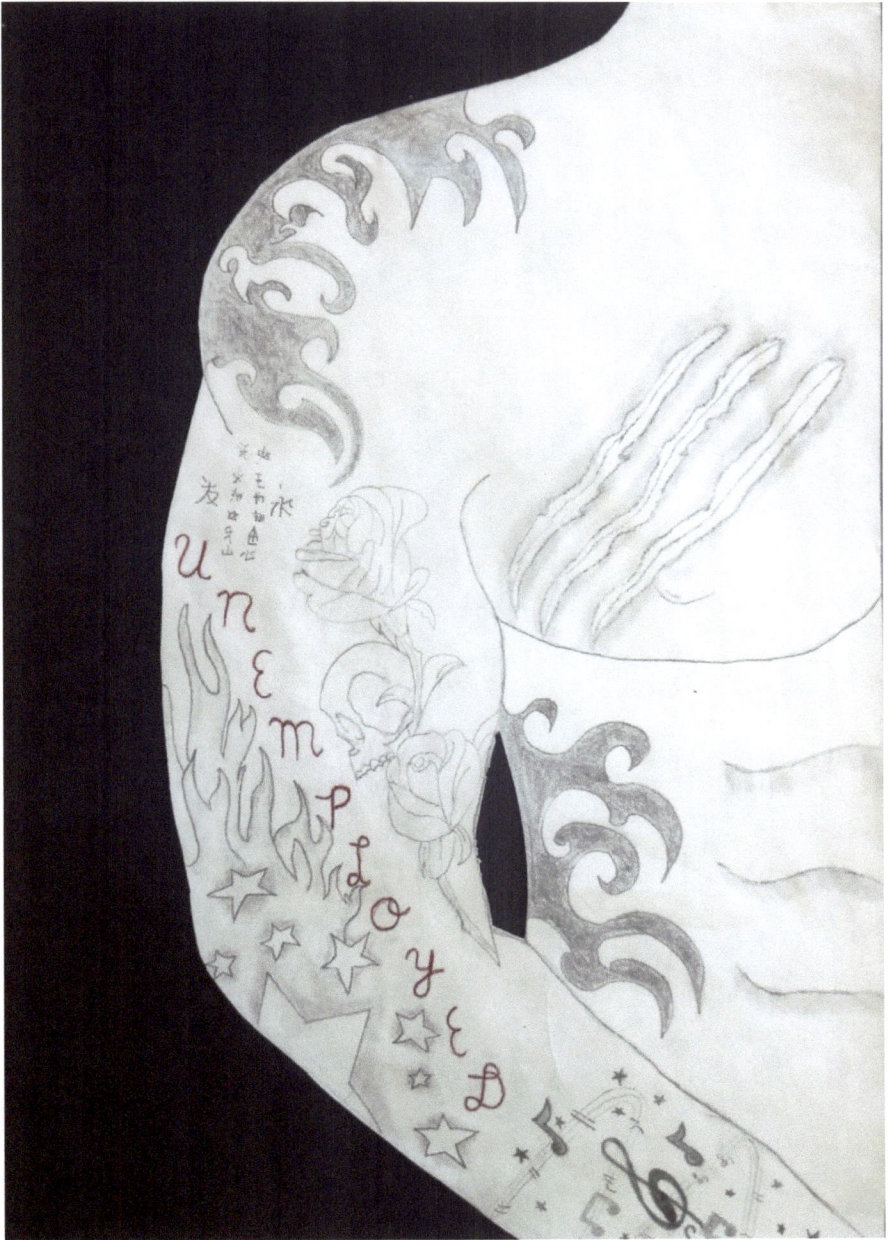

*Don't critique or correct the child's art. Color, form, spelling or subject often may not be "accurate" but is always important to expression of feelings, thoughts, situations and issues.  Mastery is rarely a therapeutic goal, but often comes naturally over time.*

This is hard for many adults. Part of art therapy training addresses this very topic – the difference between reflective response and critical analysis. If it is a challenge for art therapists, it is understandable that other grown-ups might find it difficult.

One of the most confusing and conflictual situations arises when an "artistic" child or child who is "good" at art makes art that is not technically well rendered. Therapeutic value always takes priority over artistic accomplishment.

*Meet with your child's therapist alone at least once a month. If you are a teacher or other supportive professional, be available for communication and collaboration. Your input is invaluable to your child's progress.*

This is a time to discuss concerns, gain insight, and learn new skills. Many of the things found in this book can be elaborated upon, practiced, or reinforced during these consultation sessions with the child's art therapist. It is also a time to give the art therapist feedback about how the child is doing at home or at school, in social settings, or in relation to the original reason they came into therapy.

# Part 5 – What Happens After Therapy

## Closure

Closure is as important as any other part of art therapy. Saying a proper goodbye is not only polite, it solidifies the work a client has done and reinforces the significance of the therapeutic relationship.

Sometimes it isn't possible to plan for an ending to a child's therapy, but adults can help by supporting the process when there is ample time to prepare. The art therapist will likely have a plan for closure based on the readiness of the child client.

Closure (sometimes called "termination" in traditional, adult talk therapies) involves a process of evaluating where the child or teenager is compared to where he was when therapy began, reflecting on the time in treatment, and looking to the future.

When discussing closure, the child/teen client and his or her family should know what to expect. Generally, a specific time period and an end date is set. This stage of art therapy involves a frank discussion about the reasons therapy began and the issues identified, how those issues were addressed, and what changed. Ending therapy doesn't mean that "everything is fine" but that solid and consistent changes have been made in problematic thoughts, attitudes, and behaviors, and the child/teen client leaves therapy with skills to confront old or new issues that may (and will) arise.

During the closure stage, it is also important to identify policies about contact with the therapist and returning to therapy in the future should issues come up.

Art made during this period often centers around the total time of treatment and the relationship built between the child client and the art therapist. Themes reflect contrasts between "then and now" and symbols of hope, strength, resilience, and containment.

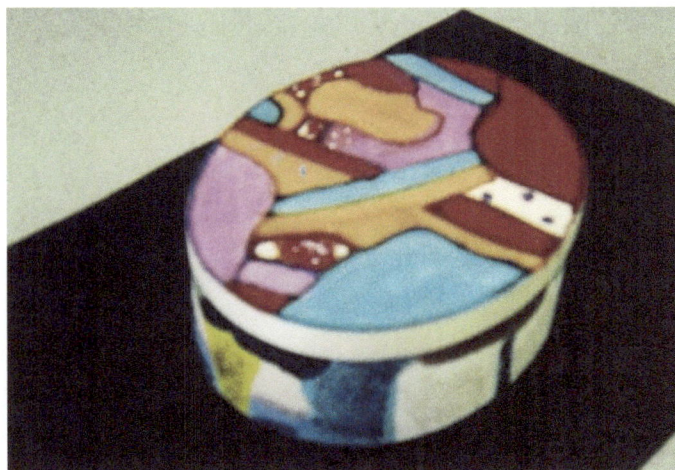

### Continue to nurture the seeds planted in therapy.

After therapy concludes, encourage the child in your life to continue using the skills she has learned.

Setting aside a specific time to talk about things which might have been topics of therapy assists a child to understand even though therapy has stopped, growth hasn't. Encouraging the continued use of art can help facilitate this.

Some families may want to set up space and material for art making. Others may want to have a few basic supplies on hand. On the next page is a list of art supplies that are pretty easy to find and accumulate.

*Good pencils*

*11 x 14 Drawing Paper*

*Crayons – fewer colors in good shape are often more important than many colors that are broken*

*Markers*

*Colored Pencils*

*Acrylic Paint*

*Construction paper*

*Modeling Clay*

*Oil and chalk pastels for older children who may have more exposure to and control over art media*

*Safety scissors*

*Glues*

*A variety of magazines, bits of wrapping paper, old greeting cards, stickers, fabric swatches for collage*

*Glitter*

*Found objects such as rocks, leaves, twigs, and acorns, small plastic toys such as soldiers, firefighters, animals, etc.*

*Extra-large manila envelopes or portfolio to store the art work for privacy and safe-keeping*

*If issues resurface or new ones arise, it doesn't mean that the child has regressed or is starting from scratch.*

It's not uncommon to check in with a therapist after therapy has ended. Often one or two sessions is all it takes to put things in perspective again. If a child or adolescent asks to see their therapist, if possible, make an appointment as soon as possible. Even if there doesn't seem to be an immediate crisis, it is good for a child to see that the adults in his life are attentive and responsive.

If a child is exhibiting old behaviors, suggest they might want to check in with his art therapist. If they say no but it seems like a good idea, remember that sometimes adults need to make decisions for children and teenagers. Make the appointment. The art therapist will take it from there.

## *Each stage of life may present new challenges.*

Even if there has not been an incident or a situation which stirs up issues originally brought to therapy, new stages of life may present new opportunities for continued growth and understanding.

A child may enter therapy at five years old and make great strides in controlling angry outbursts. At twelve, the same child may find herself using food to stuff her feelings of frustration or rage.

Anticipating the need to return to therapy at different life stages can decrease unrealistic expectations and make it easier for a child or adolescent to recognize changes in him or herself. It also makes it acceptable to ask for help no matter how old a child is.

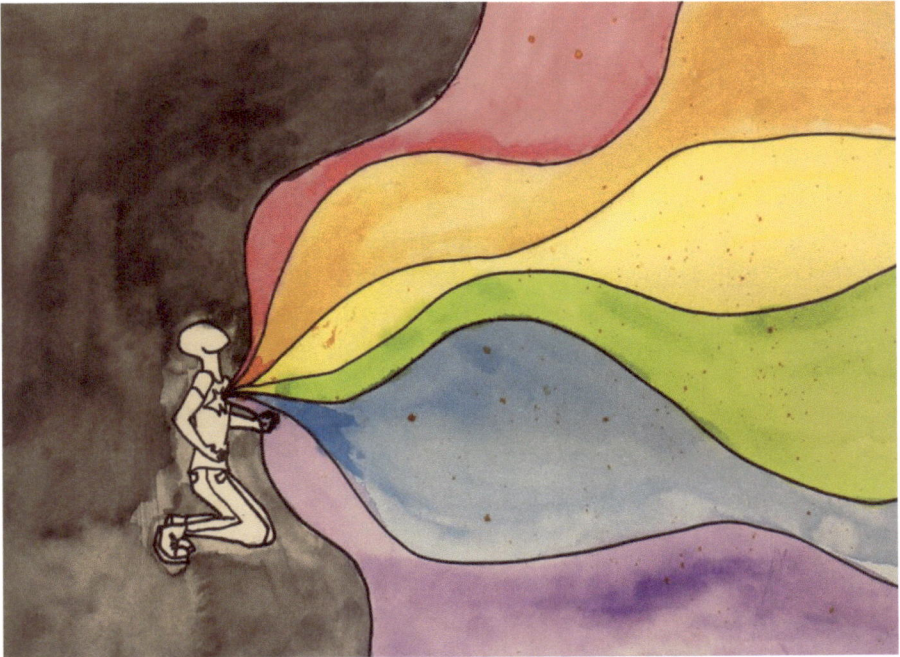

# Part 6 – Some Important Things to Remember

- Art therapy is a specialized practice. An art therapist should be properly trained and credentialed. It is always okay to ask for documentation of schooling, certification, continuing education and experience.

- An art therapist does not have "dual relationships" with his or her clients. This means that they will not be friends with the child or the family outside of therapy. This can be difficult or confusing sometimes, especially in small communities, but it is best that boundaries are clear so that the therapy takes priority.

- An art therapist is bound by professional duty to maintain client confidentiality unless he has a signed release to exchange information. When working with children, the parent or guardian must sign the release. There are a few exceptions to this.

- An art therapist is a mandated reporter. This means s/he is legally bound to report any type of child abuse and neglect or to the authorities. The art therapist also has a professional "duty to warn" which means that any risk of harm to self or others must also be reported. These are among the few times that client confidentiality can and must be broken.

- It is never okay for an art therapist to touch a child or adolescent in an inappropriate way. An art therapist should never hit, shake, slap, or physically harm a child in anyway.

- In rare instances, a child may need to be restrained in order to protect from self-harm. In these instances, the art therapist should be trained in how to properly restrain a child.

- It is <u>never</u> okay for an art therapist to be sexual with a child or teenager.

- If an art therapist has been physically or sexually inappropriate, it is best to call authorities immediately rather than confront the therapist.

- Art therapy is a process. Each child and each therapist is different. Together child client and art therapist will work at an individualized pace.

- Although training and experience may be similar, art therapists vary greatly in their approach and style. Creative therapies draw diverse therapists.

- Sometimes when a child is working on his or her issues, grown-ups realize they have some issues of their own. Therapy artwork sometimes illustrates this suddenly and unexpectedly. If this happens, seek therapy of your own.

- Art therapists work with adults, too!

# References

American Art Therapy Association, *Fact Sheet*, Washington, DC, April 2013.

Anderson, Kim L. *Culturally Considerate School Counseling: Helping Without Bias*. Thousand Oaks, CA: Corwin Press, 2010.

Axline, Virginia. *Play Therapy*. New York, NY: Ballantine Books, 1969.

Betensky, Mala. *Self-Discovery through Self-Expression: The use of Art in Psychotherapy with Children and Adolescents.* Springfield, IL: Charles C. Thomas, 1973.

Camilleri, Vanessa A., ed. Healing the Inner City Child: Creative Arts Therapy with At-risk Youth, London: Jessica Kingsley, 2007.

Case, Caroline and Tessa Dalley, eds.. *Working with Children in Art Therapy*. New York, NY: Routledge, 1994.

Gil, Eliana. *The Healing Power of Play: Working with Abused Children*. New York, NY: The Guilford Press, 1991.

Kramer, Edith. *Art as Therapy with Children*. New York, NY: Schocken Books, 1975.

Kramer, Edith. *Childhood and Art Therapy: Notes on Theory and Application*. New York, NY: Schocken Books, 1979.

Malchiodi, Cathy. *Art Therapy, Children and Interpersonal Violence*, Psychology Today, October 2013.

Malchiodi, Cathy, ed. *Medical Art Therapy with Children*. London: Jessica Kingsley Publishers, 1999.

Moustakas, Clark. *Psychotherapy with Children*. New York, NY: Harper and Row, 1959.

Naumburg, Margaret. *Dynamically Oriented Art Therapy: Its Principles and Practice*. Chicago, IL: Magnolia Street Publishers, 1987.

Rubin, Judith. *Child Art Therapy: Understanding and Helping Children Grow Through Art*. New York, NY: Van Nostrand Reinhold Company, 1978.

www.arttherapyblog.com

## Contributing Artists

*Dominique Anderson*

*Caroline Barron*

*Lennon Benben*

*Noah Bennett*

*Max Boctor*

*William Cradock*

*Eva Solome' A. Davis*

*Ellie Dillon*

*Jerry Frantz*

*Jackson B. Gregoire*

*Avery Haden*

*Stella Henline*

*Joseph Jones*

*Trip Keersemaker*

*Samantha M.*

*Meredith Shannon Murphy*

*Caroline Otto*

*Maggie Pole*

*Ricky S.*

*Dempsey Schroeder*

*Charles Stewart*

*Jane Upmeyer*

*Veblin Vermilyea*

*Monte' Weaver*

*Mance Wilson*

www.ingramcontent.com/pod-product-compliance
Lightning Source LLC
Chambersburg PA
CBHW041226270326
41934CB00001B/21